The Little Book

of

SCOTTISH MEN

Deedee Cuddihy

First Published 2008
Copyright©2008 by Deedee Cuddihy

No part of this book may be reproduced,
except for short extracts for quotation or
review, without the written permission
of the publisher.

ISBN 978-0-9551960-3-4

Published by Deedee Cuddihy
10 Otago Street,
Glasgow G12 8JH, Scotland

Internet research by Rosie
Murray

Design assistance and printed by
The Copy and Print Shop,
Gibson Street, Glasgow

Front cover shows Clanadonia performing on
Argyle Street in Glasgow

This book is dedicated to Scottish men everywhere - and the women who have to put up with them.

INTRODUCTION

It was four in the morning when I went into labour with my second child. My husband was asleep in bed beside me, our young son asleep in the room next door. Having phoned the hospital, who said they'd send an ambulance, I dressed as quietly as possible and packed my bag. Hearing the ambulance draw up in the street outside, I said goodbye to my still snoozing husband and started tiptoeing out the door. "Deedee" he whispered sleepily from under the duvet. I paused, wondering what tender words of encouragement I was about to hear from my loving partner. "Can you turn the light off on your way out?" he asked.

Of course, he made it to the hospital in plenty of time for the birth but while gathering material for "The Little Book of Scottish Men", I found myself wondering if my partner's supremely practical reaction to a highly emotional occasion was due to his maleness (a typical case of "men are from Auchtermuchty, women are from Auchterarder") or his Scottishness?

For the fact is, the Scottish male has been landed with more apparently inherent character traits than any other group of blokes on earth. Englishmen, for instance, are said to be loud; Americans - even louder; Spaniards - macho; Scandinavians - depressed; Italians - love their mums. And so on.

Scottish men, on the other hand, are (reputedly): tight-fisted, aggressive, drunken, unromantic, monosyllabic ... And then there are the negative characteristics...

The truth, as I discovered, often turned out to be far from the stereotype. But the journalist's modus operandi of never letting the facts interfere with a good story, coupled with the desire to produce a book that could be filed under 'humour' on the shelves, means that I've deliberately played up the stereotypes.

In fact, it wasn't that hard to uncover real life instances of unhealthy eating, over drinking, under emoting and not using two words where one - or none - would do.

But the stereotype that really didn't stack up is the one that Scotsmen are most famous for - meanness. My research showed that, in general, the Scottish male may be thrifty but he's not particularly tight-fisted. (Unless, of course, he's an Aberdonian farmer. . .)

Although the vast majority of anecdotes in this collection are light hearted, there is some serious stuff in the mix, as well as a nod to the 'darker' side of the Scottish male psyche. But even there, you may notice a glimmer of the humour that is usually never far from the surface, no matter what subject is being discussed with the typical Scottish man.

Most of the material in "The Little Book of Scottish Men" is contemporary but there are some historical references, too. You couldn't, for instance, produce a book about Scottish men and not include the Scotsman that one of my female contributor's has described as a "babe magnet" - Robert Burns.

MONEY AND THE SCOTTISH MAN

1. "I can't see why any organisation needs to buy paperclips. Every morning when you open your post, you get a letter with something clipped to it. All you have to do is take the paperclip and put it in a drawer and you'll never need to buy paperclips again." (Money saving advice from multi-millionaire Scottish entrepreneur, Duncan Bannatyne in his autobiography "Anyone Can Do It")

2. I met my husband at college and I never let him forget the time my sister was visiting me and he invited us to the pub where he bought both of us a half pint. On the way back up the road, after we'd dropped her at the railway station, he asked me for the money for her drink - which had cost the equivalent of about 20 pence!

3.   There's a joke I heard when I was wee and it was that copper wire had been invented by two Scotsmen fighting over a penny.

4.   I took part in a long distance rowing event that a Scottish ex-pat was in charge of and we wondered why he was so reluctant to give us our life jackets. It turned out he wanted to keep them in new condition so he could sell them after we got back.

5.   Scot Kenny Richey is putting his Death Row uniform up for sale on Internet auction site eBay. Richey said that the sale of the uniform which could fetch thousands of pounds, was: "just me getting back at the prison authorities for all my years behind bars. Call it Richey's Revenge."

6.   Donald Duck's rich Scottish uncle, Scrooge McDuck, has been added to a city's list of famous citizens. Glasgow laid claim to the miserly cartoon character, who has often been portrayed diving into a swimming pool filled with his own cash, after an obscure US comic book was unearthed proving it was McDuck's home town.

7.   Workers at Scone Palace have reacted angrily after being told that the traditional free scone they enjoy with their daily tea break is to be axed by millionaire landowner, Lord Scone, the 8th Earl of Mansfield. The Earl, Scotland's 93rd richest man, refused to comment on his decision to stop the free scones for workers, a tradition dating back many years.

8.   I once shared a flat with a bloke who was very proud of a pair of 'new' shoes he was wearing that he'd found outside at the rubbish bins. When I pointed out that one of the shoes had a hole in it, he said that

was okay because if he stepped into a plastic bag before he put the shoe on, his sock didn't get wet.

9.   Slippers owned by Sir Walter Scott are expected to fetch around £5000 at auction in Edinburgh this weekend. The slippers were gifted to the famous writer in 1830 after visitors to his home in the Borders were dismayed at the sorry state of the ones he was wearing.

10.   I started going out with this Scottish guy in America that I met over the internet but I decided not to see him again, even though he had a fabulous accent, because he seemed a little "over concerned" about money - specifically: hesitating to pick up the check for a cup of tea and a glass of wine I drank on the two dates we went on. When I told him why - he called me a gold digger! Ouch!   (From the internet)

11.   Aberdeenshire farmers are probably the meanest men on the planet. There is an expression about people who are tight with their money which goes: "Every penny a prisoner" and that just about sums them up.

12.   A mechanic who was told by one of the directors of the company he worked for in Aberdeenshire that he and his colleagues should do what they did on his farm and "go round the back of the sheds if they were that desperate for the toilet" has been awarded £16,000 by an Employment Tribunal in Dundee. The Tribunal heard that there were only three working toilets for male employees and a fourth toilet was unusable because it had a broken sewer pipe.

13.   Growing up in America, I don't remember a lot of talk about people being tight-fisted with their money. But when I moved to Scotland, one expression that I heard men use regularly in a jokey kind of way was that such-and-such a bloke was so

mean: "he could peel an orange in his pocket." It was actually a couple of years before I figured out what that meant.

14.   The Scottish men I've gone out with never let me pay for anything - not even a drink.

THE SCOTTISH MAN AND HIS PANTS

15.   I used to go out with this guy at art school but really went off him when I discovered that he wore hand-me-down underpants passed on to him by an older cousin.

16.   "Men should be very careful what pants they wear that are going to be taken off." (Advice from Scottish Daily Record Agony Aunt, Joan Burnie)

17. "I'm Scottish, so I've always regarded underwear as optional." (TV presenter, Gavin Esler talking about pants)

THE SCOTTISH MAN WITH NO PANTS

18. I was at a wedding where the groom was wearing a kilt - with no pants underneath, as it turned out. When the photographer started taking pictures after the ceremony, he got the groom to sit on the bride's lap for a 'fun' shot and when she stood up, there was a skid mark on her dress!

THE SCOTTISH MAN AND SOMEONE ELSE'S PANTS

19. In the dressing room after a match had gone wrong, the Scottish manager of

Manchester United, Sir Alex Ferguson - famous for his angry outbursts - aimed a violent kick at a laundry basket, causing a pair of underpants to fly out and land on a player's head. Too terrified to move, the player sat with them on as the manager raged. When he finished, Ferguson noticed him and said: "And you can take those f****** pants off your head. What are you playing at, man?"

FOOTBALL AND THE SCOTTISH MAN

20. "Some people believe football is a matter of life and death. I can assure you it is much, much more important than that." (The late Bill Shankly, legendary Scottish manager of Liverpool Football Club)

21. "You can handle the despair; it's the hope that destroys you." (Scottish football fan after another bad result)

22.   A Scottish football fan endured a six-day journey home after losing his passport - and seeing his team thrashed 5-1. Nick Baxter, 25, ended up taking four planes, four trains, three car trips, two bus rides and two taxis to watch Aberdeen lose to Bayern Munich.

23.   I was in hospital having my first child and the labour was taking so long that I was asked if I wanted a television brought into the room. I said no because I didn't want any distractions but there was a big international match on - with Scotland playing some team or other - so my husband, who's a big football fan, said: "I think that would be a really good idea." After they wheeled the telly in, the staff drifted away because it was obvious they weren't going to be required anytime soon. Then suddenly my husband jumped up from his seat and started punching the air, shouting: "Yes! Yes!" The midwives came running back in, expecting to find that the baby had made a dramatic

appearance - only to be told by my ecstatic husband that Scotland had just scored a goal.

24.   Back in the '60s I went out occasionally with a guy who really liked football and he invited me to a match which turned out to be the big Celtic v Dukla Prague one in Glasgow. I had no idea it was supposed to be such a big deal. Anyway, at half-time I suddenly became aware of this river of what I thought was water streaming past our feet and I looked around to see where it was coming from - I thought maybe a pipe had burst somewhere. And I saw all these men facing the back wall of the stadium and realised they were all having a pee! It was literally like a waterfall coming down the steps of the stand we were in. And I said: "My God - look! Those guys are all pissing. That's absolutely disgusting!" My friend looked really embarrassed that I had called attention to it and told me to keep my voice down. Then the match started again and anytime Celtic looked like they were

going to score a goal, the man beside me - who was a complete stranger - tried to grab me and kiss me. When I objected, his pal said: "Don't mind him, hen. He's just excited."

25.   I was travelling down to Newcastle last week on the train and when we stopped in Edinburgh a whole load of East Coast Tartan Army blokes got on, carrying boxes of beer (you could tell they were East Coast because of their accents and the use of words like "ken" and "boy"). They were en route to Paris for the game. They looked so good in their kilts and the blue and white Scotland tops. They were very funny, of course. One of them was telling a story about a "boy" who had visited a lap dancing club and he said: "£800 quid for a girl sittin' on yer knee? You'd want something 'all-inclusive' for that money!"   One of them was on his mobile to somebody and he kept saying: "Y'er a fudd!" to whoever he was talking to. (I assume it was a bloke!) Another one was practising his french: "J'ai trente et

six ans" he said to himself and then started singing the Edith Piaf song, "Je ne regrette rien." (from a letter)

26.   It's a long way from Scotland to the Super Bowl but Greenock-born Lawrence Tynes was the toast of New York City last night after helping his team to the "greatest upset" in the history of American football. The New York Giants 'stole' the SB title from the New England Patriots, thanks to a dramatic 32-yard field goal from the Scot. Tynes brother Mark, serving a 27-year sentence for drug running, watched the game from inside a Florida prison.

27.   "Scottish football remains the greatest soap opera in the world." (Football commentator, Chick Young)

28.   The importance of football in Scottish life is reflected in this joke that was going around years ago. A guy is filling in an application form for a job and in the space

where it says "name two referees" he automatically writes: "Tiny Wharton and Jack Mowatt" - both of them famous Scottish football referees.

29. Ally's Tartan Army (1978)

We're on the march wi' Ally's Army,
    We're going tae the Argentine,
And we'll really shake them up,
    When we win the World Cup,
'Cos Scotland is the greatest football team.

THE SCOTTISH MAN AS BRAVEHEART

30. "You're nae hitting the polis, mate, there's nae chance. Glasgow doesnae accept this; if you come tae Glasgow, we'll set aboot ye!" The now famous warning issued by John Smeaton following the terrorist attack on Glasgow Airport on Saturday, June 30, 2007. Smeaton, then a baggage handler at the airport, was having

a cigarette break when he heard a commotion by the main departures entrance. People were screaming and there was a car in flames. As he ran to help, Smeaton saw one of the men in the car get out and hit a policeman so he came to the policeman's defence by kicking the assailant. He wasn't alone. 'Me and other folk were just trying to get the boot in and some other guy banjoed him,' he explained. Smeaton was later publicly thanked by Prime Minister Gordon Brown who declared him a national hero.

31. Madame Tussauds has decided against commissioning a waxwork of Gordon Brown - for the time being. It says at present there is not enough public demand for one. Commenting on the snub, a spokesman at Conservative HQ said: "I guess Madame Tussauds don't want to scare their young visitors - or perhaps they've decided that he won't be Prime Minister for very long and isn't worth wasting money on."

32.   "It was announced yesterday that Stevie Fullerton, the last of a generation of Scots who rallied to the banner of Republican Spain, had died, aged 88. Mr. Fullerton was the youngest of 500 Scots to join the International Brigades when Spain's democratic government faced defeat. Speaking of his experiences several years ago, Mr. Fullerton said: "I felt strongly about the terrible things that were happening to the people of Spain. It was as simple as that. I felt if there was anything I could do, then let me do it. It was one of the world's great causes of the last century."

33.   "Aye, fight and you may die. Run, and you'll live... at least a while. And dying in your beds, many years from now, would you be willin' to trade ALL the days, from this day to that, for one chance, just one chance, to come back here and tell our enemies that they may take our lives, but they'll never take... OUR FREEDOM!" (Mel

Gibson as William Wallace in the film "Braveheart")

OR NOT BRAVEHEART?

34.   A new BBC series is set to debunk some of the 'myths' of Scottish history. It will chart the nation's progress over the past 2000 years and will show up "Braveheart" William Wallace as a failure who only won one battle. Said Ted Cowan, professor of Scottish History at Glasgow University: "William Wallace was made into a famous hero by Hollywood but many of his contemporaries thought he was an embarrassment, a failure and a nuisance."

HUMOUR AND THE SCOTTISH MAN

35. I saw a member of the Scottish band, Arab Strap in the toilets of a club and I asked him if he was who I thought he was, and he said "yes, but I'd rather not say too

much while my dick's in my hand." I said fair enough and left.

36.   Scotsmen do have an odd sense of humour - and it's even odder in the Highlands and Islands. I lived on Arran for years and I remember one day going to get some messages at the local shop which was quite a trek from my house. I'd got what I needed and was half way up the road when I heard the shop owner calling to me. "What do you want Tommy?" I yelled back but he just shouted to me again. So I turned around, thinking that maybe I'd forgotten something. But when I got to the shop he said: "Where would you be now, Jean if I hadn't called you back?" "What?" I said. "Where would you be now, Jean if I hadn't called you back?" I was so mad I could have hit him - it was his idea of a joke.

37.   Scottish humour, owning to the inclemency and the uncertainty of the weather, owing to the hardness of the soil, and the difficulty of its due cultivation,

was severe, and had always in it a certain "tang" of bitterness. Scottish humour was very largely based on the irony of life. (report on a lecture by the Rev. John Watson in Edinburgh in 1896)

38. "So Kenny Richey's Death Row suit is up for auction on eBay? I hope he's had the troosers cleaned since the time he was just an hour away from execution." (Metro letters page)

BOOZE AND THE SCOTTISH MAN

39. Calls are growing in Poland for a ban on 'men in skirts' because drunken Scottish flashers have been upsetting locals. Agnieska Gaspar, 23, from Krakow, said: "You can't go round the corner without seeing a Scot showing off what he has under his kilt while one of his mates photographs him. I saw one lying in the

gutter the other day with his kilt round his waist. He was drunk, and it was freezing cold - I am surprised he did not get frostbite." Poland has become a major destination for UK tourists mainly attracted by the cheap beer.

40.   Standing your round in the pub is something that is still very important to most Scottish men. As a child, I can remember my father regularly complaining about one of my uncles - my mother's brother - who would always disappear when it was his turn to get the drinks. It infuriated my father so much that, by the time I started going to the pub, I was already very aware of the etiquette of buying a round.

41.   A Scottish beer named as the favourite tipple of fictional detective Inspector Rebus has become a hit with US drinkers. Deuchars IPA, brewed in Edinburgh, could be on the cusp of global success after a promising trial in America. The speciality cask ale secured its place in

literary history after Scottish author, Ian Rankin wrote it into his best-selling crime series.

42.   Jim Lambie, 2005 Turner Prize nominee and stalwart of the Glasgow art scene, is talking sambucas with Toby Fletcher, owner of the Modern Institute gallery in Glasgow. "Keep it to three and you're fine, any more's a bad idea." How many did Lambie have last night? "Oh, only three. But about 15 vodkas and 20 bottles of beer," he laughs. (Serena Davies)

43.   When talking with a Scottish driving instructor, Prince Phillip reputedly asked him how he managed to keep the 'natives' sober long enough to pass the examination.

44.   A man who let off a barrage of fireworks in the foyer of a police station was jailed yesterday for 60 days. The 42-year-old walked into Alloa police station

two hours before the bells on Hogmanay and lit the blue touchpaper on a box of "300 Shot Screaming Missiles", then waved at the CCTV camera as he ran out the door. The man's lawyer told the court that his client, who had been drinking all day, had some fireworks left over from Guy Fawkes' Night and had "formed the opinion that it would be amusing to set them off in the police station."

45. I Belong To Glasgow
(Will Fyffe)

I belong to Glasgow,
Dear old Glasgow toon;
There's somethin' the matter wi' Glasgow,
For it's goin' roon' and roon'!

46. Billy Connolly drinks several cups of tea every day and enjoys them immensely although tea is only his second favourite beverage - his first choice would be alcohol, which unfortunately he's no longer allowed, as he drank his share all at

once, not knowing it was supposed to last him a lifetime.

47. Ian Rankin drinks Irn Bru two or three times a week, and he believes that you can tell a lot about a person by their favourite tipple. Inspector Rebus, for example, drinks pints. There's not much that Ian would never drink, though the warm bottles of screwtop Lambrusco which seemed so decadent to him as a teenager at parties are now, hopefully, a thing of the past.

48. "To the men of the company I will make no apology. Your husband, who insisted on me drinking more than I chose, has no right to blame me. And the other gentlemen were partakers of my guilt. But to you, Madam, I have much to apologize." (Letter from Robert Burns, 1794)

THE SEXY SCOTSMAN

49.   If Burns was alive today, he'd probably be called a "babe magnet." He loved women and they loved him. It's been said that one night with Burns was worth a life time with an ordinary man. (Elspeth King.)

50.   "In books, the image of the Scottish hero is a sexy one, and it takes a special kind of woman to tame him. But he has a loyal side, too, which you can see in the Scottish clans. That kind of extreme loyalty is very appealing to women readers." (Karen Kosztolnyik, senior editor at Warner Books in New York)

51. "Scottish men are so passionate and uncontrollable. Just the thought of trying to tame one makes me feel weak at the knees." (from an online chatroom)

52. "Dear Sean, Still think you are the sexiest man alive - next to my husband!" Janet, Cleveland, USA (from Sir Sean Connery's official website www.seanconnery.com)

53. I lived in London for years and when I got back to Scotland I was struck by how good looking Scottish men were. They're much sexier, too. But with Scottish men, there's a shocking lack of looking after themselves which is maybe why they don't mind getting into fights. I think there's also a feeling of wanting to belong to a group or a clan and being very loyal to that group. Or am I just talking a load of bollocks?

54. VisitScotland is calling for eligible Scottish men who think they've got what it takes to attract single women to Scotland. And with the search now on to find the twenty 'hottest Scots', players from the Scotland rugby team today took time out

of training to be among the first to sign up for the campaign. Denise Hill for VisitScotland said: "Women across the globe love Scottish men – the kilts, the accents, the sense of humour. It's a fact." Scotland and Glasgow Warriors prop, 26-year-old Euan Murray, said: "I'm really keen to get involved in this campaign. I'm sure there'll be some tough competition but I'd be delighted to be one of the Hot Scots!"

55. Hi! I'm an American girl and I have an offer from St. Andrews University, to study Art History, but I have never been to St. Andrews - or any part of Scotland. SO... the question that's been bugging me is: what do Scottish lads look like? For the ODDEST reason I have this idea of them all looking like Jake Gyllenhaal. Hmm.. not that he's even remotely Scottish. So you see why I need help!
(Question on an internet forum)

* Half of them look like Mel Gibson in Braveheart and the other half look like Ewan MacGregor in Trainspotting.

FOOD AND THE SCOTTISH MAN

56. We went to this hot food van really late one night and most of the guys in the queue seemed to be getting something called a "Scoobie Snack" which was two fried potato scones, two sausage links, a slice of Lorne sausage, a hamburger, two pieces of bacon and a fried egg, all jammed into one roll. One of the men who was waiting for a Scoobie Snack said: "It tastes even better with mustard squeezed on the top."

57. With regard to Scottish food and the alleged consumption in Scotland of deep fried Mars Bars, I would just like to say that the deep fried Mars Bar was apparently invented by an Englishman who ran a fish and chip shop here.

58. My husband is a Shetlander and enjoys cooking. He's a real mutton and potatoes man but he'll use parts of the sheep that even other Shetlanders don't eat anymore such as the bottom end of the leg, bits of the belly and the kidneys and heart. One day he brought home a plastic sack with six sheep heads in it but ended up using only the tongues.

59. My Uncle William was a bit obsessive about his food and insisted on having the same meal when he came home from work. As soon as he got in, he would sit down at the kitchen table and my Aunt Margaret would give him his tea. It was always mince, boiled potatoes and baked beans. He would put HP Sauce on all of it and then prop a comic - the Hotspur or one of those little Commando comics - up against the sauce bottle and read while he was eating. After the main course, Aunt Margaret would bring in his pudding: custard with tinned fruit; either mandarin oranges, peaches or apricots.

60. A guy I used to share a flat with could only cook two things: baked potatoes with muesli and spaghetti with mustard.

61. I had an uncle whose favourite snack was biscuit sandwiches - specifically custard creams crushed between two slices of white bread.

62. Death Row Scot, Kenny Richey, 43, says he can't "wait to get home to Edinburgh" to taste his mother's cooking. "I've dreamed so long of this moment" he said. "My ma's tatties and mince was a favourite of mine and I used to think about it a lot - if only to drown the taste of the dreadful prison food."

63. My boyfriend had just moved into his first flat and he invited me around for dinner. As soon as I walked in the door, this horrible smell hit me. When I asked

him what it was, he said: "Kipper Surprise" which turned out to be spaghetti bolognese made with a kipper instead of mince. He was so chuffed that he'd invented this new dish that he made it every week for months.

64. My father, Frank was a big fan of one-pot cooking. When he was living on his own, he'd come back from the pub on a Saturday afternoon with a good drink in him, having bought, on the way home, a boiling chicken and a mixed bag of carrots, turnip, leeks and onions - as well as a quarter bottle of whisky. He'd fill a big pot with water and put the chicken in, along with the vegetables which, although cut up, he wouldn't have washed or peeled. Then he'd sit down in front of the telly, drink his quarter bottle and fall asleep. By the time he woke up, the food was ready and he'd eat the chicken from the pot with his fingers, leaving the 'soup' for the next day.

65.   This guy I had been seeing for a while offered to make me dinner one night at his flat. I said 'great' but when I arrived he put a plate of beans-on-toast in front of me. I said: 'Where's the dinner you promised me?' and he said: 'That's it' and was really surprised that I wasn't dead impressed. He said it had taken him ages to make.

66.   "I like to try and keep busy. I've got interests in lots of things. But one thing I'll say about life is - you can't beat a good fish and chips."   (Big Issue seller, Neil McLauchlan)

THE SCOTTISH MAN AND TOO MUCH FOOD

67.   Scottish men are significantly more likely to have the most dangerous form of obesity than those south of the border, according to a new study which shows that

the belly size of a typical Scot is "significantly" larger than their counterparts in England and Wales. Said Dr. Fraser McLeod, primary care lead clinician on Glasgow's Diabetes Managed Clinical Networks: "Scotland is facing an obesity time bomb and we cannot sit back and watch this happen. Nobody seems to recognise the consequences of the beer belly."

68. Healthy eating campaigns are doomed to failure because many Scottish men would rather have a figure like Rab C Nesbitt than Ewan McGregor, according to new research.

Scientists found that a large number of the Scottish males they interviewed prized their beer bellies because it meant they did not look weak. The trend was so pronounced, according to the study, that some men of 'normal' weight even wanted to be fatter. The research was carried out on 80 shift workers who were shown a series of drawings of a male figure in his underpants, starting with a skinny

physique with protruding ribs and hip bones, right through to a grossly overweight body shape with a big beer belly. Despite a culture full of images of slim movie stars, models and musicians, all of the men picked as their ideal body shape one of the pictures showing a clinically overweight male.

69. A labrador from Hamilton in South Lanarkshire has been named "Pet Slimmer of the Year" after losing more than 20 pounds. Oscar had got so fat from munching sausages, roast chicken and pasta that he collapsed under his own weight.

THE SCOTSMAN AND HIS KILT

70. Kilts weren't fashionable in the 1950s when I was growing up but my mother used to send me off to the Sunday School

every week wearing a full kilt outfit including a jacket, a sporran with tassels on it and shoes with buckles. But the worse bit of the outfit were the matching tartan underpants - we called them breeks - that I had to wear with the kilt. So that was itchy wool material right next to your skin. They were quite tight, too so it was hellish having to sit with those on every Sunday. No wonder I don't like kilts - or religion. Maybe that's why Scotsmen are so aggressive - it's a throw back to the days of jaggy underpants. Another problem was my cousin, who didn't have to wear a kilt, calling me "kiltie, kiltie cauld bum" whenever he saw me in mine.

71. I'm from a Sikh family and my impression is that Scottish Sikhs are more Scottish than English Sikhs are English. Maybe that's because the Asian community in Scotland is smaller. A lot of us wear kilts at weddings, for instance. When one of my uncles moved down to England, I noticed that he played up his Scottishness. His Scottish accent became more

pronounced - to the extend that some people said they couldn't understand him! And he makes a point of talking about Scottish teams when football results are being discussed.

72.   It's a funny thing but as soon as a Scottish man puts a kilt on, there's a transformation. They suddenly become more masculine - and more Scottish - and acquire a kind of swagger which is odd because you'd think that wearing what amounts to a skirt would have the opposite effect. It's a bit like a woman putting on high heels and a sexy dress.

73.   Are all Scottish men ugly or is it just most of them? And wearing skirts is unreal. Why can't they lose the skirts and the bad language and have face lifts or at least get spot cream? (question on an internet forum)

* Nine out of 10 Scotsmen are pig ugly - it's the inbreeding. And men wearing

skirts is just pathetic. You'd think when you are that ugly, have an awful accent, pale complexion, GINGER hair . . . the last thing a man with any brains would do is wear a skirt!

* Seriously mate, can you not think of anything else to talk about? This from a man who is the same nationality as Dean Gaffney? From a country where Wayne (Shrek) Rooney is considered an icon!!!! Scots men wear kilts 'cos they have such large penises they cannot be contained in their trousers!

ROMANCE AND THE SCOTTISH MAN

74. Friday night is very much 'love night' for the Scottish man. Arriving back from the pub, having partaken of the traditional Scottish aphrodisiac – 12 pints, a black pudding supper and 3 pickled onions - his mind is set on just one thing. . .

75. "Went to a great private view on Friday night. Lots of interesting looking people, including an actor - stumpy, dark haired, middle-aged Scottish guy . . . plays a policeman (oh, YOU know!) - with very tall, red haired girlfriend in high heels. Last time I saw 'stumpy' he was with said girlfriend in the middle of a Tracey Emin exhibition, groping her bum (I think it was a first date)." (From an email)

76. Scottish men are quite good at buying jewellery for their wives. When a man who had already bought a lot of gold bangles for his wife came back to the shop for another one I said: "Has she got any space left on her arms?"

77. A' coorse a love ye darlin', Ye'r a bloody tap notch burd,
An' when ah say ye're gorgeous, A mean iv'ry single word.

So yer bum is oan the big side, A don't mind a bit o flab,
It means that whin am ready, There's somethin' therr tae grab.

So yer belly isny flat nae merr, A tell ye, ah don't kerr,
So long as when ah cuddle ye, A kin get ma erms roon' therr.

Nae wummin wha is your age, Hiz nice roon' perky breasts,
They jist gave in tae gravity, Bit ah know ye did yer best.

Am tellin ye the truth noo, A nivir tell ye lies,
A think its very sexy, Thit yev goat dimples oan yer thighs.

A swerr oan mah grannies grave noo, The moment thit we met, A thocht ye wiz as guid as, A wiz ivir goanie get.

Nae maitter whit ye look like, Ah'll aywiz love ye dear,

Noo shut up while the fitba's oan, An' fetch anither beer. (Anonymous)

78. Green grow the rashes, O;
Green grow the rashes, O;
The sweetest hours that e'er I spend,
Are spent among the lasses, O.
 (Robert Burns 1787)

79.
Oh, I love a lassie,
A bonnie, bonnie lassie,
She's as pure As the lily in the dell,
She's as sweet As the heather,
The bonnie purple heather,
Mary, ma Scotch blue bell.
 (Harry Lauder)

80. I was matched up with a Scottish guy on an internet dating site and after we had emailed back and forth a couple of times I gave him my phone number. He called up and we discussed the possibility of meeting up when he next came to London. He mentioned that he smoked dope and

that he liked going to pubs and I said, well, I don't smoke cigarettes or dope and I don't drink, either. There was a pause and then he said: "Well, I hope you masturbate." At that point I realised I probably wasn't his type after all.

81. I used to go out with a bloke who delivered coal for a living - which shows you how long ago it was - but he was a real charmer. I was really worried about my weight at the time and I remember him saying to me: "My God, if you get any thinner you'll disappear when you turn sideways." I knew he was lying but it still made me feel better.

RELATIONSHIPS AND THE SCOTTISH MAN

82. I had a German girlfriend who seemed to need regular reassurances that I loved

her. I said: "Look - I told you I loved you months ago so assume that I still do until I let you know otherwise." Eventually she went off with an English guy.

83.   A man who was charged with the attempted murder of his estranged wife walked free from court in Edinburgh yesterday after being admonished on a reduced charge of breach of the peace. The 33-year-old pled guilty to driving his car without due care and attention while his wife was on the bonnet, causing her to fall off.

84.   "She was close to her father who, being a Scot, did not express his depth of feeling, but she had an incredible bond with him."   (Charles Jencks, speaking about his late wife, Maggie Jencks, founder of the Maggie cancer care centres)

85.   When my father finished his meal at night he would burp - quietly - and then

say: "If that's my dinner, I've had it." I think it was a kind of 'veiled' compliment to my mother on the quality of the food she had produced. But if he didn't like the look of something, he would just say: "No" and she'd scrape it into the bin and make him something else. It was a very traditional Lanarkshire relationship but they loved each other to bits.

86.   When I was at uni I went out for almost six months with a girl I didn't fancy at all. I asked her for a date when I was drunk and although I realised my mistake as soon as we met up a few days later, I didn't want to hurt her feelings so I carried on seeing her. Our last date was at the pub on Valentine's Day, which I know is the worst time you could pick to dump someone but I had finally met another girl I really did like. To make matters worse, the girl I was dumping had got me a card and a box of chocolates. Not only that, I had no money so she had to buy the drinks. After a couple of pints, I told her I'd met someone else, said I was very

sorry, then left. I was absolutely starving so I took the chocolates with me and ate them back at my flat.

87.   My ex-husband was so bad at communicating that he left it to a removal man to tell me our relationship was finished. In the middle of buying a new flat, I discovered he was having an affair but he swore it was all over and that he would never see her again. On the day of the move, about a month later, I went on ahead and he made some excuse about staying behind to "tie up all the lose ends."   The removal men had shifted almost everything into our new flat, apart from my ex's clothes, books, records and painting things - he was an artist - and when I pointed this out, one of the men said to me: "The gentlemen told us to take his things to another address." It turned out the affair wasn't over and that he was moving - not to our new flat with me - but to her place. We never spoke again, except through our lawyers.

THE SCOTTISH MALE PSYCHE

88. "Down-to-earth and matter-of-fact, he had all the good Scottish traits." (Racing driver, David Coulthard speaking about the death of his friend and colleague, Colin McRae in 2007)

89. Maybe Scottish men are a little afraid of change but apart from that they're refreshingly normal. They say what they mean and they don't take themselves too seriously - and I'm very happy that I married one.

90. "Forget 'Begbie' in the film "Trainspotting" with its stereotypical images of miserable and violent locals. Scots have survived English invasion, brutal weather - and the pain of having the world's worst goalkeepers - to see their country become a top destination for

visitors to the British Isles because of the warmth and friendliness of the welcome they receive." (From the Lonely Planet Blue List in 2008)

91. "Glasgow comedian, Frankie Boyle also asserted that Scots can be a rather negative lot, and cited John Logie Baird who, when people came up to congratulate him for inventing television, used to grumble: "Aye, but there's f*** all on!"
(Brian Viner)

92. Charlie and Craig Reid warned that Scotland's macho culture is partly to blame for hundreds of people committing suicide every year, around 75 per cent of them men. Charlie Reid, who has himself battled depression, said: "There is still a big macho culture in Scotland, men are particularly bad at not showing their feelings. I'm still guilty of that. There is an attitude that we should just get on with things and stop moaning." (The

Proclaimers at the launch of "Suicide Prevention Week" in 2007)

93.   On the eve of an Old Firm clash against Rangers at Ibrox, Celtic manager Gordon Strachan has revealed that a fear of failure drives him on ahead of every game. Strachan said: "I worry before every league game that my team could get beaten. I have a fear of getting beaten. I don't fear anybody but I do fear getting beaten and I have done since I was a kid."

94. "Wee Jimmie Krankie" has been voted The Most Scottish Person in the World by readers of the Herald.

95.   I consider myself a man's man. I've done, and do, all the 'man's' things. But now, in my later years, I realise that the little handful of really true, loyal and supportive friends that I have are all females. So that must say something about Scottish men - although I don't quite know

what!"   (Jimmy McGregor, musician, writer and broadcaster)

96. What marks a lot of Scottish men out from other men is an ability to laugh at themselves. It's their saving grace. They like to think they're 'hard men' but that often falls apart when they've been drinking and, God help us, become maudlin, sentimental and patriotic.

97. My father-in-law had a horror of being conned. If he thought my husband had been "taken for a ride" over some transaction or other - had paid over the odds for something, for instance - he would say "You were done" or "You mug, you."

98. When I was growing up, you would never see a man in Scotland pushing a pram. That was women's work. My father would only go to the shops in extreme circumstances and he would never take a

message bag with him. If he had to buy a loaf, he'd have it tied up in a brown paper parcel before he'd carry it up the road.

99. I've never dressed up in Scottish battle garb or kilt but my grandparents on my mother's side are Scottish. My mom doesn't have an accent, she just has a red face, a nasty temper, likes to drink, play golf and have a good time - like any other true Scotsman! (Mack Palhemys talking about the background to his film "A Scottish Tale")

100.   Could the English possibly have prospered without the Scots? It was, after all, a Scot who founded the Bank of England. And it even took a Scot to write the words of "Rule Britannia".   (From Burkes Peerage and Gentry)

101.   I resent it when people come up to me just to be rude about my work. Why do they feel the need to say: 'That film was

rubbish'? It happens a lot in Scotland. (Ewan McGregor)

102.   "Then the realisation dawns. The slagging is not just part of their competitive nature. It is a part of them being Scots. It is a national trait that we show our love by giving out verbal abuse. The higher the level of slagging, the greater the depth of love. They are brothers, after all." (Hugh MacDonald interviewing the tennis playing brothers, Andy and Jamie Murray.)

103.   With Scottish men, if they slag you off it means they like you. My girlfriend isn't Scottish and she used to come back from the pub almost crying some nights and say: "Your friends must hate me, the way they were slagging me off" and I'd say: "No - it means they like you!" If you haven't seen someone for months you don't say: "I've really missed you; it's good to see you again." You say: "How

are you doing, you old bastard!" It's a sign of affection.

104.   The "Atonement" star, James McAvoy, lives in a tiny second-floor flat and drives a battered Nissan Micra worth less than £1000. The 28-year-old Scot remains devoted to his un-starry roots with his modest home in Stroud Green, a far-from-fashionable area of North London. (Heat magazine)

105.   Scottish "Dr. Who" star, David Tennant, 36, refused to say whether he has signed up for a future series of the show and revealed that he wasn't 'bovvered' that Catherine Tate's character, Donna Noble - his assistant in the programme - doesn't fancy him. He said: "Not being fancied just reminds me of being back in school, so I'm used to it!"

106.   When I was 16 I started going out with a guy called "Chip" who did look a bit

like a chip but he was 24 and worked as a plumber and had a car so I was quite chuffed that he was my boyfriend. I decided to bring him home one night to meet my family and they were all sitting around watching the telly. My mum let him sit in her chair and half way through the programme we were watching he stood up, cocked his leg like a dog and farted. Then he nodded over at my dad and said: "Good airse, Tam" - obviously referring to the fart. There was a stunned silence, because no one ever farted out loud in our house, and then my dad - who was quite a refined man and was always called Tom and never "Tam" - got up and walked into the kitchen, motioning for me to follow him. He just looked at me and said: "Get him out of here now." I walked back into the sitting room and said: "We've got to go Chip." And that was the last date I had with him.

107. Men in Edinburgh are quite reserved; in Glasgow they're outgoing and gregarious - more like they are in Liverpool, where I

come from; Fifers are really tight with their money and in Ayr they're all mental.

108. The image of Scots that Harry Lauder portrayed to the world: drunk, tight-fisted with money; a hairy kneed, sheep shagging, hielan' haggis catcher in a shabby skirt - probably put this country back at least 50 years and lingers to this day like a bad smell. (from the internet site FirstFoot Hall of Infamy)

109. I go to France a lot on holiday and men there don't seem to be as aggressive and macho as they are in Scotland. As soon as I get back home I can feel the tension - even at the airport. Or maybe it's just Glasgow.

110. I was in Paris last week and what really struck me was how openly affectionate men were to the women they were with. And I mean couples of all ages. You hardly ever see that in Scotland. I

don't think my husband would even hold my hand in the street.

111. My son was given a Timmy Tears doll for Christmas one year when he was about three and he had it with him when we were travelling through to Edinburgh on the train. An elderly man passed our seat and when he saw the doll he stopped and said: "Fancy a wee boy with a doll. That's disgusting!"

112. A female chartered engineer whose career dreams became a nightmare when she returned to Scotland for a job, claimed at an Employment Tribunal in Glasgow that male line managers at the company she had worked for made personal remarks about her sex life; expected her to do the work of three men and suggested that she could be asked to provide cover in the company's reception area.

113. In my mid-50s I began to experience a certain level of what would probably be called "erectile dysfunction" so I went to my GP. He immediately started writing out a prescription for Viagra and when I said to him: "Do you know if it works?" he looked really affronted and made a point of letting me know he had never had to use it himself - although he was at least 10 years older than I was - but his patients had told him it was very effective.

THE SCOTTISH MALE PSYCHO

114. I can't turn to friends and say: "Read this, it's really good. It's about a bloke who gets drunk, gets a kicking off the police, goes blind, then spends the rest of the novel wondering why his girlfriend left him and where his tobacco has gone." (a review of James Kelman's Booker Prize winning novel of 1994, "How Late It Was,

How Late" - the one with all the swear
words)

115. "Frank, the 16-year-old anti-hero of
Iain Banks' debut novel The Wasp Factory,
was born and raised into a hugely
dysfunctional family on a remote Scottish
island. Deserted by his mother, ignored by
his father and with a brother recently
escaped from the secure hospital where he
has been confined for setting fire to dogs .
. . " (from a review)

116. Justice Secretary Kenny MacAskill has
called for early kick-offs at important
Scotland football matches to cut alcohol-
related crime. He said: "It's not just Old
Firm games where kick-off times are
important. I was at the Scotland-Italy
game where we didn't get the result we
wanted but we know ambulance call-outs
went through the roof immediately after
the match, as did domestic violence. That
wasn't because we had lost. It was

because people had been drinking too much all day."

117. What has surprised me since coming to Scotland from Cameroon is seeing a man hitting a woman in the street. Even more surprising is seeing a woman hitting a man. You would rarely get that in Cameroon; women are more respectful there - at least in public. But the people I'm talking about had all been drinking.

118. The gory legend of Sawney Bean and his infamous family of 15th century cannibals - claimed to have butchered up to 1000 people during a 25 year reign of terror along the Ayrshire coast - has been dismissed by a leading historian at Glasgow University as "political propaganda by the English." Said Fiona Black: "Cannibalism has a long history as a means of political propaganda used by a dominant culture against those they want to colonise. As an English invention, Sawney Bean may have been written to demonstrate the savagery

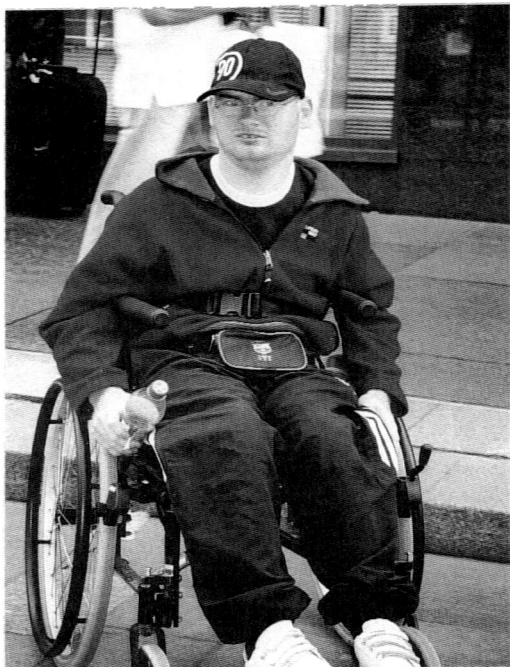

and uncivilised nature of the Scots in contrast to the superior qualities of the English nation."

119.   Back in the 1970s, Dundee was the worst place to visit. I went up there with a boyfriend for the day and we went into a pub in the city centre and the reaction from the all-male clientele was like something from the Wild West. The place went completely quiet and everyone turned around and stared at us - and not in a friendly way, either.

120.   A 36-year-old Perthshire man attacked a total stranger and knocked him unconscious in the street - for being from Dundee. The man, who was under the influence of drink or drugs, had been hunting for Dundonians in the minutes leading up to the attack which took place on St. Valentine's Day, a court was told.

MacGAYNESS

121. Scotland is great for gay men - all those kilts and hairy legs!

122. Andy Murray has achieved No. 1 ranking in the world as the tennis player most fancied by gay men. Apparently this is due to his boyish looks and "a degree of vulnerability - because you never know what injury he is going to get next," according to the gay dating agency that conducted the poll.

THE MODERN SCOTTISH MAN

123. I've got two kids with my second wife and I look after them as much as she does. Our daughter is only a few months old and I usually take her out in a baby carrier, strapped to my chest. Every once in a while I've been caught short when I've been out with her on my own and have had to nip into a public toilet for a pee. No one standing beside me at the urinals has ever made a comment about it. I suppose that's a story I'll be able to tell her when she grows up!

124. Modern Scottish men are completely different to what they used to be. One of my friends gets a staff discount where she works at Marks & Spencers and I said: "You must be able to get a lot of nice things for your grandson" and she said: "I wouldn't dare - his dad is very particular about what he wears and he would just bring them back." And the wee boy is only five!

SCOTTISH MEN ON BEING SCOTTISH

125.   I think I'm very Scottish and I'm discovering each day how much more Scottish I am. As the variety of apparent choices in life open up to me, I realise how few of them are real choices. I just go on doing the things I always did and these things seem to be governed by my origins. (Alan Sharp, writer)

126.   "I've never liked nationalists. And the anti-English thing in Scotland has acquired a nastiness in the last 10 years that I hate. To imagine for a second that you're endowed with certain attributes because you come from a certain geographical point? It's shite. Hitler would have been proud of you." (Billy Connolly, interviewed by Brian Viner)

127. I don't think Scottish men are particularly aggressive, they're just more direct and to the point which can be intimidating to some people. Wanting to 'cut to the chase' is a cultural thing which can be misunderstood.

128. "Maybe it's part of the Scottish inferiority complex that we try harder to make our name in the world. In motor sport, we have punched way above our weight and it boils down to us wanting to be taken seriously and do things which will make other Scots proud of us." (Sir Jackie Stewart, racing driver)

129. I don't think Scottish men are very good at small talk. I don't think we really approve of talking unless it's to say something meaningful. You really notice the difference when you go to England where they seem to be able to chatter away for hours about nothing - literally. And in Scotland you're taught not to call attention to yourself so it's quite difficult

when you're trying to get into acting, which I am, and you have to go to auditions where the whole point is to show off and demonstrate that you really are the best person for the job. But I think that's changing now. Scots, in general, are feeling a lot more confident. I'm not a nationalist but since devolution, I definitely feel more proud of my Scottishness.

130.
Oh, but let me tell you that I love you
That I think about you all the time
Caledonia you're calling me
And now I'm going home.
If I should become a stranger
You know that it would make me more than sad
Caledonia's been everything
I've ever had.

("Caledonia" by Dougie MacLean)

LANGUAGE AND THE SCOTTISH MAN

131. A friend of mine who doesn't think he has a very strong Scottish accent was visiting New York for the first time and was really insulted when this guy he was speaking to said: "What part of Poland do you come from?"

132. "The Russians are wonderful at languages. They say the late Czar prided himself on his good English, until he found when he came to England that, having learnt from a Scotchman, he spoke Scotch . . . " (Beatrix Potter writing in her diary in 1882.)

133. "The Scots language prefers understatement to elaborate declaration. Confronted by Helen of Troy, the most beautiful woman in the world, a Scotsman might have said, "Aye, no' a bad-lookin'

wumman." " (William McIlvanney writing in the Sunday Herald.)

134. When I first came over to Scotland from Denmark, men would occasionally say to me "You're not a bad looking woman" and it was a long time before I realised they were paying me a compliment.

135. American presidential hopeful, Hillary Clinton, addressed the question of what the first-ever male "First Lady" might be called when she appeared on a chat show last week. "His Scottish friends have been suggesting 'First Laddie' " she revealed "but I'll just keep calling him Bill."

136. "Clash the pans, Sadie, we're a' hungry." (From Archie Hind's unfinished novel, "Fur Sadie")

137. "Alba gu bra!" ("Scotland forever!") - Mel Gibson as William Wallace in the film "Braveheart"

138. Jings! Crivvens! Help ma Boab! (Oor Wullie)

Acknowledgements

With many thanks to: Darren Smith, Charlie
Murray, Chris Cuddihy, Anita Leslie, Bob
Cuddihy, Avril Paton, Elspeth King, Fiona
McIntosh, Lis Nicholson, Anita Manning,
Manjeet Sagoo, Clair Scott, Mikey Cuddihy,
Dave, John McHugh, Tom Murray, Hope
Singleton, Jimmie Macgregor, Jean, Rosie
Guy, Paul Holleran, Elaine Scott, Ann
Donaldson, Charles, Robert Cherry, Iain
Scott, Ann Marie, Jack, Rebekkah Linton
Gillet, Alison Hutcheson, Scottish Metro,
The Independent, The Sunday Herald, The
Glasgow Herald, Ken Smith in the Herald
Diary, Joe Lau, Kevin Meehan and Mavis,
David Macaffer, Jonathan James Patterson,
Allan Ballingall, Thomas McLaughlin, Mark
Foye, Joe Gough, Raman Sandhu and
everyone else who contributed stories and let
me take their picture. Plus Ray Grant in
Alberta, Canada who emailed me the
following joke:

A Scottish soldier in full dress marches into a
pharmacy to speak to the chemist. The Scot
opens his sporran and pulls out a neatly folded
cotton bandanna, unfolds it to reveal a smaller

silk square, which he also unfolds to reveal a condom. The condom has a number of patches on it. He holds it up, and eyes it critically.

'How much to repair it?' the Scot asks the pharmacist.

'Six pence,' says the pharmacist.

'How much for a new one?'

'Ten pence,' says the pharmacist.

The Scot folds the condom into the silk square and the cotton bandanna, places it in his sporran and marches out the door of the pharmacy, kilt swinging. A moment or two later the pharmacist hears a great shout go up, followed by an even greater shout. The Scot walks back into the pharmacy, and again speaks to the pharmacist.

'The regiment has taken a vote,' the Scot says. 'We'll have a new one.'

About Deedee Cuddihy

Deedee Cuddihy is a journalist who was born
and brought up in New York but has lived in
Glasgow since the "Big Storm" of 1967
(which she slept through). Or was it 1968?
After finishing art school in Glasgow, she
realised being an artist would be too difficult
- and being an art teacher would be even
more difficult. So she became a journalist
and has been one ever since. She is married -
to a Scotsman - and has two grown up
children. "The Little Book of Scottish Men"
is her fourth book. Her first three
publications were "How to Murder a
Haggis", "The Little Book of Glasgow
Jewellery Stories" and "Dog Vomit on
Toast" the last of which was not a runaway
success (maybe something to do with the
title?) which means there are loads of copies
left which she is willing to let go of very
cheaply. Maybe even for free. So get in
touch if you want one.

Also by Deedee Cuddihy

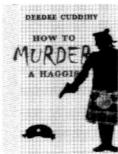

"How to Murder a Haggis" – a sporran sized collection of real life haggis stories and Burns Supper disasters.

Buy "How to Murder a Haggis" by Deedee Cuddihy direct from the author for £4.99, FREE postage and packing in the UK. Send cheques, payable to 'Deedee Cuddihy', to Deedee Cuddihy, 10 Otago Street, Glasgow G12 8JH, making sure to include your full name, postal address and phone number. For sales outside the UK, email: deedeecuddihy@aol.com or write to the above address.

Praise for "How to Murder a Haggis"-

'Proper out-loud laughs' - *Avril Paton*

'A lovely wee book' - *Matthew Perren*

'Hilarious!' - *Murdo Morrison*

'A splendid feast of real life haggis horror' - *Fiona McIntosh*

'Great Stuff!' - *Ray Grant*

'Do you think you'll ever write a book that somebody wants to buy?' - *author's daughter*